PERENNIAL FASHION   PRESENCE FALLING

perennial

fashion

Fred M

Moten

presence

falling

WAVE BOOKS
SEATTLE / NEW YORK

Published by Wave Books

www.wavepoetry.com

Copyright © 2023 by Fred Moten

All rights reserved

Wave Books titles are distributed to the trade by

Consortium Book Sales and Distribution

Phone: 800–283–3572 / SAN 631–760X

Library of Congress Cataloging–in–Publication Data

Names: Moten, Fred, author.

Title: Perennial fashion : presence falling / Fred Moten.

Other titles: Presence falling

Description: First Edition. | Seattle : Wave Books, [2023]

Identifiers: LCCN 2022045157 | ISBN 9781950268801 (hardcover)

ISBN 9781950268764 (paperback)

Subjects: LCGFT: Poetry.

Classification: LCC PS3563.O8867 P47 2023

DDC 811/.54—dc23/eng/20220926

LC record available at https://lccn.loc.gov/2022045157

Designed by Crisis

Printed in the United States of America

9 8 7 6 5 4 3 2 1

First Edition

Wave Books 107

flyboy

art in motion
sister yam

full mantis

lateral agent

they call me
common wind

contents

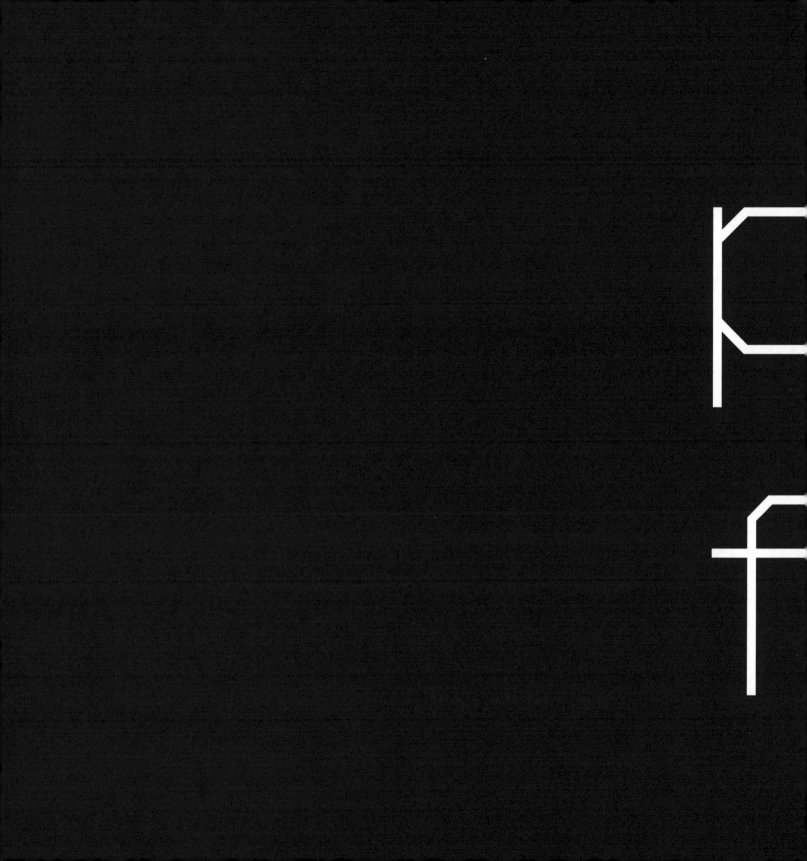

the red sheaves

we're walking
an open diary.
inconstancy,
which seems
like exercise
in parting,
is really
overlap
and incline,
a velvet
soundmap
of approach
inviting
sublorn
attention
in approach
to write the
movement
of our viewing
in the moment
and apply and
violently to
soften our eyes
as she applies
and softens
brightness and
shadow in
emulsion, grave
and fly in rough

compliance,
sharing trembling
cusp in tending
unknown partners,
toward them
as we practice
saving differences
in quiet stride.
should we
take off
our shoes?
may we take
off our shoes?
touring
this mosaic
of fluid,
thickened
planes,
loosened
as we keep
turning cube
in continual
return of
leaving being
sensorium's
variorum,
to scratch
and spin still
being stranger,

in that manner,
with those
manners,
lightly measured,
somehow
mistaken,
the sharpness
of these angles
lets us gently
ply the angles
of our turning,
almost trying
to get behind
the volume
of the room.
there's warmth
there, where
they seem to
come from.
they are
recording
angels, so
we join them.

them, now, what are
they, these surfaces or
garments, or tapestries,
or sculptural afformances,
whose shade and weave
refuse the mix of prior
separation? it's not that
they're not paintings;
it's that in that they are
painting's not what it is.
cranky intelligence,
running all the while
from what he stomps on,
hiding dancing cheek
to cheek in brutal murder
petting brilliant dogs,
says they're jazz, or
jazzy, in regard of
brutal, tentative regard
of brilliant fullness
in the ethical expanse

of our intensity of touching.
but no one ever occupies
their own space darns that
dream of subjects holding
objects in their hands.
the open-handed
sow all that
away, aside in
seeding, releasing
into turbulence,
to which close looking
opens, listening to linen
run and cluster. attune,
and the room is not a
volume but a way, some
surfacing, unit caught up
in playing back diffusion,
where we follow
with our fingers'
eyes, tracing the retracing
of our steps, while
light that's always
been in there comes in.

"my surfaces
are the extent
of my reach."
stay here. her surfaces
aren't flat if you move
slow, step to and from them
as you're in them,
them all trance in
transit indicating all
against held still in
holding, surfacing.
all over ain't the same
as all up in, a black
and red sea'd haptic
operation, seeing
reverently seeing
ceding refuse to
accede to observation,
exuding plaid in the ongoing
making of an atmosphere in
rubbing, leaving pouring
from the wall in tinted,
slightly tented fabric. sea,
ms. jones? a book whose
pages wash long shores.

look how we get a depth-feeling of words on leaves. but what's a depth-feeling? a variant on, or a vagrant all up in, a picture-feeling? is it glad, man? is it sad? is it three-dimensional emotion? a feeling of it—which is softly unillusion, imperspective, anoptic trick in actual travel, someplace to dance and tarry where the words make thunder in the air— might drive you mad, man. open blocks, or boats, or text ferrying knots between foam and dry. can they be staggered, torqued, quadrilateral in turned through the difference on their margins? the dream would be a way some blocks might verge in the ardent grids of eye tests, to get the feeling of a structure always verging, having always deserved writing, as if writing be walking back and forth to turn some air on in the room, or turn the ground over, or turn jewels into motion on the wall. the stroll, while we stay here, is cursive, and suddenly trance is torn, and then there's tearing.

and what about this
nonsensual semantic
phenomenon in which
the word "constant"

in the phrase "constant
structure" can only ever
mean to change? change
is syntactic substrate, so
that "constant structure"
is what we errantly keep
calling, in echo of our
blessing, changing
same. delta sustained,
all blue, be laughing at
decision. meticulous,
we share the concern
de le métèque pour
the meticulous, whose
presence welcomes
gentle, urgent,
outdoor deviations
of the sea.

                              we constantly
want   in tonebursts,
structure out of
                              round   laugh, delay,

and jackie-ing march,
   where some same
qualities with different
   roots play parallel,
   giving free and shifting
nothing eccentrinsically,
nonsensually depth-felt
   in being seen + heard   but cool
   to be more + less than   in how to
reason comprehends,   stay

   in how we just can't stay
         and how we can't just stay.

                              oooh, a structure of wind
                                 or a range of absent
                                 wings or tongues that
                                 keep on making their
                              impression, o, afterparty
   of apprehensile coil
   recalling bird, as some
      birds recite aesthetic
   enformality without an
      art form or an artist
   or a balloon released
   that we all be driving,
      but all held, but all
      flowering hedge.

if we take some notes to cull into a row of breathing, can we see they won't quite fit
that tore up edge, wrapping 'round pages past euclid and queensbridge, sunk in the nasty
implications of our points and lines, the neighborhood they refer to in shook turn, which gets to another
cousin of constant structure, the logic and the graph of place themselves, in their destructive play on plotless
selflessness maintained in folding, bending, crumpling, and tearing, too, and acute, and fine as hell,
and constantly, endlessly, shouting carolina in the general blue, in grass, and must be abstract, too.

feeling-depth is soulful
refusal to separate
practice from what
that was in your hand.
nothing ever comes
of infinite rehearsal;
we preface what we
practice all along,
writing laborious
weaving's aerate blocks
and thread and patched
murmorial quilt, post-
woven, bent gee and haw's
remorseless visiting and
working, more tilling,
more tiling, grounding
improvision, uprooted
roots up under a table
prepared for revising.
this steady occultivation
of nothing in general,
in black refusal of the
cult of genius, which
black geniuses keep
trying to renew, keeps
wandering as they keep
wondering, dread looking
back while laying back in
lightly hoeing rows in all
that yearning in your hand.

how many consecutive
chords can we play?
we need constraint
so we can see a layout
of what ain't been laid
out yet, a remnant
of all but conceived,
a shadow of indication.
let's see what it's like
to submit to no design,
undevoted to line breaks,
only come from being
broken, when we come
upon what comes up on us
from behind, when we're
walking straight ahead,
eyes wide open, over the
rent-partying cliff of some
striving cliff as we curve
through the bend in the
river, in the shimmering
moonlight, and the water,
remember, and the birds
and the sharing attention
and all the ledges, as if
all y'all been waiting for
we and dem, we'n'em,
in the general guianas.
remainder, overlooking

bridgeless gray in the
edge of eyes whose edge
are blue with age and fall,
raise, foregiven as the sea,
the ravaged and the loved.

the book is a three-
dimensional scene of
     our infinitely rich
and more unruly free-
dimensional jam, don't
feel bad, it's a volume,
          and a room   ,   but the page
is a plane, it's just plain,

          brocaded nonlocale
spread out from our
turning, through a kind
of rising,   past the term
of that lonely binding
into anapolymer. the
                    bright read extent of our
reach beyond grasping

is what abstraction is supposed to give, what imaginary numbers give
in how we work through
little play
complexities
by obstruction,
so we get to
go through someplace else

as something comes for us
in all this goings on, until we
surface-feeling-depth in our
complicities of the
book party,
in the book of riot,
in the general chicago,
because it lets you see better,

the music's
residue
lets you

hear better when
you go outside
and matter builds
from groove and shift to
gather, for tonight
we are the book, we are
the field we are.
not what we are,

in sedimental brooks with open gales, with no name all involved with singing with, with just with comping, withal with weaving with the work of come and go, we make believe in differing till we believe in surfacing, in sounding, and then, drawn out past every partial dignity, a song. parting is crowded in this oncoming, in this part of ungoing flow and flow, choir and quire, row and ϱ. caress, confession, congressive edge. the rim breathes. the red sheaves.

covering

in the broadest conception
of black music, which is the
truest conception of black
music, black music can't be
conceived. a music of covers,
black music covers, and cover
is nonconceptual. if you've
ever covered, if you've ever
been covered, or have you
ever been laid down, held
mutual and dappled, shift
untempered, ensemble, and
ardent in the only love,
which is incandescent hate,
so you know what covering
discovers, hands on, so what
it is to lay on—which blurs

in proximity—is all up in
what it is to approach and,
darkly, to reveal? if you've
ever wondered if it's some
wandering in covering, if in
separable is gone, to go awry
and astray and still ain't gon'
get there, and still on the edge
in wait, then you gotta want
not to get there just as bad
as you wanna get away from
here, blown back, been
studying how not to know,
unknown, black blue as black,
black burying ground, blue
as burnt black grounding in
the broadest, blackest edge.

corduroy, no strings attached,

but might be deeper in the dark
and fade, or in homer's fade to
mrs. hamer rubbed to shade in
gray, chromodyptic illusion and
subsistence and relief. the junk
house of his thoughts sits there
as a commitment, an intensity,
and become a story for all y'all.
a diver, familiar with surface's
underside, which is haywood
rivers, says the sea is interfacial
layer, as ammonites on the boat
of ra, as broken anchorites tell
a story for all y'all all all alone.

the interfacial layer
is violence and care

a breach
we make
walking

air's soft
emphasis
to send

the intrafacial lair

the malecón of
cameroon is aerosol
and ceiling, curve
and plane and hold
a little while, hiss
and thickness
in the batterie
and embouchure,
aquella boca curve
a little thick
sometimes. caress
enough release
to seethe, and sea
enough to foam and
vent, to leap and
ground and foment
agricole and massacre.
this rum of fervent
and fermentive son
is for arnelle fonlon,

who is propelled by
 sunday dinner and
 remembrane, of speech
in hearing, in fellowship
 with fools in muddy, exonymic
 wouri's scrawl and scroll.
we're too from the good
 black dirt. we're too
 from the good black
 holland houston-jones,
 whose air not in
 between is a little
history of sip and shhhh,

 some cracked, implicit
 breath still falling off
to velvet, the physical
 chemistry of the good
 black beach and bridgetown
spray and mexican diffusion.

afro-alienation lining out

bernie mac never hung out in cicero
but daphne damn near went to chitown,
summum bonum summumum bitch,
arturo! ooo wee! bertolt! bertolt! dab,

it's devastating when she says my love
is alive. her brain bleeds through his
broken organ. you say, her distancing
in our distancing is our distancing,

which we can't deserve. you mean to say
we can't deserve our we, our terrells
named secretly after tammi? really, you
can't even say thank you for listening,

no haven, nothing next other than what
we been doing, nowhere to be, nowhere
else to be, no other kinda being, just
patient cut and deepen, deep and wide.

tables and gems

held and unheld here in love, having been accused of telling stories, look how violently we fold and tint and follow haze come into branch and spring and gone and breathing armor. come make some garden inside. the scene is everyday let's see. the situation is fractured arbor. an old dress made new the old way, out of absent extra, starched and pressed in low gravy, come up on not enough again's invisible veer. plot gets folded, handed, and put away with all our fibrant things of hush and ardor.

flavor is an undertone of broken necessity. fray, as ornament and active hip, be switching toward suggestion. broke off almost all the time into break me off some, fold shades. irregular fragments of satisfaction and shine. fold, and then leaf, for these violent festivals, cooking till you can't cook no more, anthologies of disappointment as is you is until, unsettled, scene is the set of all unheld and held in pure routine. must be ours. can't be ours. must be, though, 'cause suggestion just can't stop.

so, let's prepare some impreversion, freaky seen. you see it in pursuant retrospect, p-e-c-t depicted on deep saucers, in dead clearings, where we read mistakes away in sheen from undermemorial maid preparations. we want to be ready. we got to get made up is what we got. data's allure is lore in shades and tables turn immeasurable. consoled, come set some and unsettle. come sip some. saucer start singing after all that ravishing. glaze ain't got no sense. see, that's just the glamor of suffering.

this abstract thing going abstract for you, with our built-in best visual practices, lets tables provide limitless interruptions of analysis. the rhythm of tongues lacing rice with scraps don't count. won't stop because company has its place e'ver'y once in a while. we sweeten and persuade, but don't count on that. wood unravels into juke. braided color dries and tesses. miss alma adds some leaves to read. coffee's air ain't particular. smoke hums unmade patterns of bazaar and aftervow and mutual eidh.

data fabric design and little pitter, panthers, polish, nick, and singe like schoolteachers. a pontiac and a bunch of pamphlets, some mutual shudder looking back, and little time circles listening to y'all in pain. send 'em off somewhere deadly to practice bye. the scold they've come to expect is the cold they used to feel. it's all love. it's all about love, fold, and no one survives intact. y'all gone now and the album, and that little mark he would put on what we give away, sprays out into unfamiliar hands.

in the bottom, can't be too much strife in the background, or too much shade in smoke. we need all the sunset of the color. if flames are gemlike, it's ruby duncan, my dear. all the people in the picture are the people in me. this overcrowding is all off in regular amazement from root to root, and inlaid with imaginary mill quarter body. jack fluffyscuffs on time to the splintered walls of the news of the world. so that the beauty shop, as if they were a silver platter, stay and take our seat and say, shhhh.

we're always about to hear something. what we hear is something we're all about to hear recede in plain sight and song in the sense of things, and in the way. wonder what all that wonder's about? it's about to withdraw, something 'bout to be withheld. if there's a secret in what we see, it's gone. can we go, too? let's go all up in there for the memory, for all work's intricacy on boo-boo's birthday, tintless on the underside. sometimes you be looking for the color over there and here it is, unbound.

ultimately, the rhythm is so supersessive that preparation foregoes itself in light. what's left is what wouldn't have happened. and ain't no baseline for the club's proceedings. there is, however, her shell, with its ominous protection, a rumble completely taken away from jealous hums and folded into this whole offset of cues, for the cœnobitic pleasures of cove, cells wondrously bearing both rendezvous and interview. see if we can't get you into ceta. see if baccarat can't let us be. see your

lower left arm in the lower left corner, fold? sometimes prepare is just see meadow on the wall. we love the lichen of our fingerprints when we feel them like strangers, the bloom and the blemish all epistrophic in the general catastrophe, which we meet in double sets of folded arms. am I my father in my smile? the stormy circle blessing that left corner moves from frame to frame to keep from moving. we work what's held here cosmically. the buttons, and the sewing of the binding.

another word for blur is backbone slip, or cart. various ways of going home to the way more direct gleam of palenque's isle of palms in the history of paving and stealing. the history of who was here is read as here we are. that recoil is our travelog. I wanted to touch myself along the seawall. he saw me coming from a mile away. that embrace was how we said something through one another. our hipness comes so smooth, girl, I can't believe it. I believe in it, though, though I don't get around.

this lavender blocking of the saturday dance must be a tone effect of our pan-affective turn. shit kicks in at a level of intensity that far outweighs our actual contacts. I need to see you this way, through another color, through a board of tone breathing overtone in the blocking of the village. if I see that setting, then I can see the emanation of show and fade and we have to work too hard for the beam we give back. something's wrong but we can fix it. let's see if we can fix it right now.

see how all the irreparable landscapes feel like they persist in variety? pretty soon the kids will come and take these books and records and lay 'em out in flowers on the sidewalk. even acute fingering of work and their scarved and scarred and feathered hair will disappear in the echo of what we give away, which I want to give away in echo, in the echo of an abbey, in the all and all in your hand and eye at the end of blue monk again and again and our green thought is you.

the faerie ornithologie

of fumi's

dancing

branches,

feels

the nonsensuous feel

of feeling

depth,

the range
of fringe   or frill,

the trill

that various change

of direction

makes in murmur's

various gathering of
breeze, the tinge of various

turn in murmur,

nonsense, blue

fascinum's

return to exodus,
unvoid or atom,

not between

bird
and all the various indecision.

for there
is nothing lost that may

be found if
sought is neither

here nor there

in tide and flight,

array, repose
and tarry

a triologue of sylph and soul

sylph said, naw, we selfless. soul said, shit yeah, we look back, wonder, visit whirlwind, be the dusty air we in like little violent stones, varnishing, then vanish on shore and curve and cursive and straight mumble in the prefatory secret we press down on, real quiet through sun and moon, like a sylphide etching where we whisper "etching!—recess! withdraw! erosion! nonsense!—massive fête!" while we dance while we at rest.

self, that motherfucker, said, we write that we don't have to write together. we never want to take our solemn pleasure. we write together like we don't, so what we write is barely born. self said that shit like he was sad. why we act like we ain't a band? soul said. see that? rob brown just saw kidd jordan sound like daniel carter lifted by the air he breathes. lifted out of self like soul at visiting. soul smiled, visiting our ass off is how we grind and underbreathe, off edge and ground and fly. look here, now, here we go! sylph said, in ruins, through

ruins. sylph's alternate flesh tone be brown B♭, soul said. not in between the elements of air and earth, sylph said. spirits blow real pretty but dirty, the good alert of soul in selflessness, for ruins, soul said, then here come kidd downstairs, and william said, you alright, kidd? and wadada said, he alright, he just blew his heart out. kidd's alright, sylph said, in ruins, in that windblown stance the wind blow, conquered but ain't kilt yet in the general strike of breathing, soul said, when we be kneeling, tilling, pulled, shipped, held in leaves.

sylph said, tree dance. their visit is the secret life of plants, them cutthroat palm blades. ain't nothing to get but feel, soul said, on precarious string. feel not in between touch and slash what fronds feel, hold up sever in the same breath, which sylph lays down on blue. all y'all air always be fighting, somebody said to all y'all air. somebody be saying that shit all the time and it's true. our air? soul said. that clear, brown motion kidd blow while daniel lift how we be fighting all the time? we be running through how they leave us in ruins, orange in bright red on that rock and looking for sticks. and let me say, soul said, before we say another word, that somehow you sure look good that way you visit through the wall. you visit through the wall like jeff be sensing music—seismically, sylph said, in broken strokes of pointbrush, all elvin and mysterious and mischievous indexical cyan, in that secret we all know but cyaan believe it. you mean almost to scream in ruins in deliverance of bridges as a secret structure; you mean every wordlessness in blistered, gliding, tout-monded, double- and triple-tongued mindfulness, air river, riffer, rifter of air, sylph said to soul, soul smiling all alto in the all too spiral sun.

after all is said and done, we always got something to say about sylph's grime, soul said, all that bottom in the way they breathe. sylph breathe like henry grimes, soul said, their flight like bottom land not in between your toes, tapping in and out of shoes depending on the weather and y'all weaponry. weather seem like it's always bad, sylph said. chicago just a town in mexico. we just messing with velvet, soul, said sylph, which is all we want. self don't want no softness on his hands while we be burning. let's blow that shit away.

are you
one of these
motherfuckers?

yeah, yeah, you are, and you don't seem to be tired of this
suspension, which is falling, whirling and unworlding storm,
for precision in mourning. we really don't respond to these
motherfuckers. the discipline is our imagination. the whorl
is our yardbird school, a choir of uncertain azure in scratch
galaxy, the violent measure of a gleam in her eye. you can stop
calling here for some kinda response to these motherfuckers.

what we got for y'all is precision in mourning and turbulence.
we got a way of taking substance away in circling and surfacing,
the slow obliteration of pain in pleasure, a release of coffle on
dusty highway, an ongoing unraveling of quilting. we always
got to be killing these motherfuckers in the edge of morning
after morning of absolute, uncountable new remembering.

the immediate breathes through us before anything and these motherfuckers can't understand that. we're instruments of clinical ecstasy and if you want to listen you got to give up everything. you got to give up listening to sharing in folding in the bottom in oceanic engineering in the ungrammatical suffering of scourge and smile and babies in the nonresponse.

when we salvage our surfacing and circling from your savage enclosure, it will be this miracle, right now, singing through can't breathe forever in this world and we ain't talking to you, motherfucker. it's gon' keep on being this miracle, our praise, our rite, miss pearlina, and all the thickened kitchen anarchy of our phrasing, the denotative detonation of am I blue, some times I'm blue, bye, burn, while all y'all everything be burning.

color field

in the color field there's
blood at the root. our
schedule is everyday
sunshine blood, every
dead nigger on the street
in every record spinning
around, every last one
whirling. that's what
every record records
in the blue they see.
which one of you
motherfuckers can see
and can't see that? black
arts vs. black abstraction
is a lie again and again,
like you get not to see
all that brutality in all
that blue. you don't get
to not see, motherfucker,
but what happens when you
act like you do? somebody
black and poor can't
breathe, everybody dying
of their dying breath,
nobody laying with them

on the ground, all of us
all fucked up with our
phantom child, and
you get to act like you
alive in a brutal gallery?

tiling, lining notes

a river is studio agitation through one window,
aloft in rock bottom's soft support and
    rumble, a room, a cell alight in the way the
      walls walk off in juba'd pat and tiling,

    the pattern on the river floor all absolute
and indiscernible unless you walk it, in the
    river, as the river, as all this rotary soar of
the dammed and held, sous vide in second

    linearity, parading in this tuba'd lining
out of the basic line all and against itself
in black and blue switchback and beatrice
    smiling seeing all our little differences

together in the venereal collection area's
    serial eddying of how we taste and feel,
inseparably. there's just so many ways to
    keep going along the way. the miraculous

influence is delta'd in floridian branch or
mangrove double silt, coahoma co. moaning
   or swung oklahoming—a gap band or a gap in
nature kinda sounding, drowning, burning, this

continually caribbean being on fire of the
   river, from river to river on canal and torn
      to another bleeding place we from in our
   lenape shift, our delaware gap band, sending

      geography through a sycoractic horn chart
   of the natural city in and out of its broken
      window, cadence still cruising mobile studio.
unnamed, and making waves, and making ways

is what it sounds like: lining, tiling, moaning,
   smiling, drowning, bleeding, burning, seeing,
      sending, sounding just like joseph daley,
thurman barker, dave holland, and sam rivers.

tilling, limning notes

tile, or fleck, as if
daub or stroke, but a cut
of blue, flesh cut a glance of
blue for trane,
in the general murder,
all but mute for
amadou diallo.

you have to get
so close to see the glance and shine
you get too close
to see the glint in flames, read
the braille of trembling
through the sea of inflection, éclat et clinger,
and cling to the firmness
of our wave function, a clarity
of sweep in black as dawn
dawns on us with
such gravity, such fabricant gathering
of matter in the fabricant matter
of gathering jack whitten's
rose corona, working violently
with outpouring, work
made of unmaking
a monastic love of sequence

in sequins, in solemn, intermittent
spacetime sewn with the
decorative weight of edward witten and thomas
witten and bill frank whitten.

this scroll of cut, outbroken canvas
looks like looking with a movie. injured, lined out
surface adores flatness with thick
character acting, mapping distressed by aerial
grounding, scuffed ornament, microtonal
abrasion all over again. the textural slur
of tilling and limning, emma and emily
whispering, the precise irregularity
of anamosaic gesture, is a habitat

of schools in a bessemer tree, a reef chorale
and blue hint shadow, graphic
soft enough to tess and more
and wreathe. a totem is
a haunted keyboard, and this ingenious
mechanical device is so we
can differ in elegiac practice—
for criticism is grounded
differing and deciphering is
separation's scale.

surfacing

even listening some, while walking
around, while they try to look up
close, where tutti counters under
all over like tootie heath, like the
daze in grain, the specific gorse
in specific burning, giving, glare
again from boll to wisp, which
won't be the same as centering,
surfacing can only be reviewed.
eccentric landscape and recur
misbehave two or three times
in dragged approach and blown
in common wind and broken
weather. sound like some sugaree
complications of surfacing walking
around, our boots on, and take 'em
off, and put 'em in a row on the
porch, then shell some peas off
our delicate patch. surfacing is
different than facing by surfeiting
and forfeiting the terrible history
of face become surfacing, which is
the history of position, which confers
through circle in ongoing plait. it's
closer than that. prefering surfacing
to face so close that water run like
libba's hard-row luxury,

light compression,
a tightening slice of lighted acre,
which bears the weight of our
delay. soft, breathable textile,
fibroid matt with blood from
hand in torture, all that blood
breathed by manchester babies,
all that blood drunk by the man
in mayfair, the vegetable lamb's
blood on branches, tied to the
whipping machine, trapped in
the drum machine, jewel set
in drum's whip topography,
baled in pools of blood mixed
by a pioneer, spun out by dj
gandhiji for protection and
remembrance, to demonstrate
subtle boom and fire,

to make do, and overdo,
and linger in this always being
overdue, always behind, arrear,
interred and double entered,
interminably indebted, which
seem like it do so much sharper
now than any deed for this
handing and tilling, this light
stepping on stolen land. what I
owe you? nothing, all, surfacing
all over the place, superficial, some
superfacility of passage, or passing
out past passage in surfeit, supple,
super supplement, subluxurious
wealth already given in po lil ol
making do's lil ol sharing in
coming, all forfeit in generate
handing over, in steady transgress
giving not enough, which is too,
too much.

the cotton gin
is inseparable in defacement,
in the blasted and unavailable
and disavowed portraits we let
the world see 'cause we can't look
unless we look so close it's gone
'cause we gone 'cause we gone,
in seeing all in nothing all above
and below and aside, in surfacing,
in this fiery digging and hovering
thickening surfacing in tending
to it, dubbing and redoubling the
merger and divergent complicity
emerging in the way out of no
way we keep misplacing in all
that spinning and milling around,

tilling and mixing and weaving,
that purposeless spinning and
demonstrating always about to
go off, all but out of round in
how outness is always pending
in this hanging around, this offset
setting down, always all up in set it
off, tending toward getting set out
for the new thing, looking back
and looking around and bending,
spinning hid in the work and the
wake of the southern question,
does spinning negate the careful
brutality? it's just the sunshine in
your brutal uniform.

                    all that blood
is the engine. is that gin a computer?
that computer picks cotton. all the
magic is industrial. is your mac a
mckinney? nothing is but who's
digging, granting every wish, all
this combing in soufflé, as if a
bend was climbing in the thickness
of our flagrant dream, all turned
and spun in how we're trapped in
what we need, our gathering in
hunger, our murmuring in murder,
our holding on in being held.

                    yelling
'cross that ochre field, in a tempo
we share, to turn. it's spring, and
yelling mixes, or new immeasure,
and the stripes are high-draped,
really yellow in that tender, evening
tree. what's the difference between
grounding and background? it's not
between them, but it is all up in
grounding and background, and in
their common engineering and
imagining, because the sound of a
field that's worked and played on
by a black family'n'em for a hundred
years makes owning a lie until, some
kinda way, it doesn't, in some kinda
so-called freedom, and then some
kinda way some nothing comes out
from something and plays all through
the work to play like it holds some
thing for us, for them to see, to hear
the burning of our giving it away,

                              making
                     laying sculpture down light blue,
                     like looking can't be felt but

                    sound. nobody
brought their box but they come
to see you give. they have, evidently,
so they want some more. they want
more demonstration, the circle, the salt
march, the charkha, the shaker, the güira
the engine, the garment in surfacing
sounding like groove thread burning
and giving, but it's not just that,
'cause in the touch of these tables
you prepare, surfacing curves the
convulsion of our feeling and their
looking not quite close enough,
that convolution always surfacing
again so that there's still the heavy play
of surfacing. having worked through
break and console, surfacing describes,
tells out its own ekphrastic outline
out of turn, unplotted, burned in
giving, ain't no story ever mine, ain't
no spot ever belonged to me, no
map of all the intensities of either
edge, just a spot so real that its surreal
complaint, which differential presence
brings through all that weighing, never
close enough to feel or hear or see through,
all up on you at a distance while we're
on the ground, is that we demonstrate
surviving by spinning, which is surfacing.

the abolition of art,
the abolition of freedom,
the abolition of you and me

art don't work
for abolition.
art works for
bosses, like you
and me. if "let's
abolish art" sounds
too close to "let's
abolish you and
me," it's 'cause it
is. I love art and
I love you, too,
and this is a love
song, so it's got
to be too close.
freedom is too
close to slavery
for us to be easy
with that jailed
imagining. we've
been held too close
by that too long
in all that air they
steal in our eyes
while we swarm in
common auction.
in my eyes, art had
me from hello it's
me when ronnie
isley oversays it.
I thought about

us for a long, long
time. I followed
mythic being on
the bus. if I'm a
slave to art am I
a slave to love? am
I a ferryman? am
I abridged? am I
from houston to
oakland to hugh
son to oakley to
houston to oak
land ave, or just
a name to have
for this ordered
action, no aviary
setting, just absent
settling for the
moral law within
on this highline
stroll? ain't there
this new way of
gathering that's
not like that, like
when we do it so
pretty, and there's
no selling instead
of visiting, just this
old revolutionary
visiting where no

one lives in how
we fellowship in
abolition, which is
long and sudden
presencing when
ruthie gilmore
undersays it? this
exhausted, endless
swerve of beauty
from art, of move
meant from free
dom, jail being
their being held
in being, not ours,
is way past you and
me and the lives
we hide away from
them and you and
me in looking after
them. art works their
being there. that's
the cold, funerary
origin of the work
of art. our beauty
wants to hold us
in not wanting
being there with
them, don't want
to be like that at all.

let's work on work
like murray jackson.
let's work through
work like general
baker. let's work
it and reverse it,
like ronaemedsim.
let's work against
monastic rule with
the boy next door.
let's work against
anything that works
against we jah people
can make it work.
let's work against
royalty like a prince
formerly known as
as the artist; let's
work against how
art don't work for
abolition. let's work
the artwork down
to common nub's
low gravy. let's work
through freedom
from can't see to
see through how
we mow miss lady's
yard, when we were

talking with erica,
and we talked about
toni cade bambara,
and erica held her
so soft on fire that
we saw blue fields
in june jordan's
eyes, and we saw
that we could sit
and talk about a
little culture. we
saw that we could
see through our
selves through
sylvia wynter in
america; we saw
that in broken
memory of them
we'd starved our
mothers with still
accomplishment,
drowned in real
abstraction and
false care, holding
our held against
each other for the
tired purity, for
some let me make
you over in the

image of my dream
of who I am when
I dream of being
me at the center
of all dreaming, a
circle of dreamers
of the center all
dreaming of me
in lemon yellow
sun, a picture of
another world
where you're my
residue, my love.
even in my black
art you do just
what I say till the
black aesthetic,
which black art
bears with love
and leads us from,
leads us from art
and you and me
and slavery and
freedom to afform
and oblige in
near and lovely
distancing our
real black share.

approaching

dirty south   florida water   general chicago   nigga cemetery

the consensual validity of gone off in the muck,
spread all out with style but no cloth like some
offering in our way, obscure and open if we dig
down in it soft, dirty, south all under the world,
is gone off in the national security state of virginia
whose official theorist declares method on black
skin as a manicured lawn, as an alabaster factory,
as strip mining the top of his stolen mountain,
as buck v. bell. but when billie's arm bends fumi's
note motherfuck this paramilitary weatherman

and his tired navy blue. but navy looms. when
we say fuck all that all together, he buys up all
that sound. he's a privateer made hard in the
long history of singing cargo and his hard, blue
armada shows up all over the world to scare
the shit out of people, blowing people's shit
up, blowing people up and shit, like our show
and tell and shit ain't shit, y'all. so we say, let's
take his breath away. we think our submarine
ways, breathe quilting circles, brood and caress

new technologies of rice, mulatto rice and dirty
rice and rice and peas y moros y cristianos,
some jollof jumped off jumped back through
the circuitry of thrown derivatives reimagined
in new rain, and wonder will that drown them
in our endless drowning? ain't big mama's edgy
bread o las arepas de la abuela our post-colon

art of resistance? can't the deep structure of
our food be how we were never kings, in the
flavor of our needs, in how we stretch our

need out through the way of things, like salt?
cookin's relation to moanin' has already been
established as having hurt too good not to go
over again, going 'round the way they go around
too tight in the ass for florida's general chicago,
sensing the general strike in maud and janie,
trying to narrow that down to jumpy solitude.
the general chicago of haiti is common all over
arkansas, in the travels of the women named
smith-pierre in refuge, laid in ashes, on rush

street, in the cold, specific savannah of ladbroke
grove or weeksville or bondy. can't you hear them
holding our breath in chili's sound, can't breathe
but common wind and rose water of some women
named rosewoman? if you want the feel of musical
fume, but you got here too late for them to fix you
a plate, get up early tomorrow and wait for the bus
and let them play your voice and hand it back. it's
been too long since we dreamed about that land of
california, the general chicago home sweet home

and thursday's oh so sad except the water ritual.
thrung blackbirds off-center, on central, locked
up in the parker center, at the corner of adelanto

and krome, police gone bird hunting in foshalee,
which is deeper down in florida than the fucking
muck we be musing on for our lives and their
muhfuckin' amusement, here, at this beautiful
museum. take some more black lives for us to
muse on for your fucking amusement, muhhh
fucka. national culture is financial security for

the devils of national security, making anti-muck
out of spread-out style. the irrational reproduction
of these impossible motherfuckers is spurred on by
you and me making this breathtaking shit out of the
shit we make. then, it ain't shit no more, all taken
and gone in us by us in charter at the nature theater
of the langston hughes academy of tulsa, oklahoma.
but wonder if there's one more unexploded bomb?
and what would a black female superhero do down
there, on water, when they done killed the school

with their meteorological corniness, all blue but
not the kind that's blues as we're all tangled up
in these navy suits until it seem like the general
percussive trumpet is their reveille and appetite?
look, this is about masks and weapons and the
difference between our beautiful things and what
we want from our beautiful things and what we
want to want and what we don't want to want.
somebody blew up our freedom school and sent
us to the school of the free so we could learn to

want what we don't want. when the grass is gray,
or when it's black, when I go home to kingsland,
which is cuba's bon voyage, mimi takes me straight
to the front room to play me a song and then I'm
homeless. I'm not homeless, my people still be
there, so I have a home, I'm just not there, being
not and all but held in being all but sent home to
turning through returning to buenaventura, and
don baudilio takes me straight to the front room
to whisper in my ear, in the paramilitary air, that

don temís is gone, that home is where the art is,
where the klan and their new black faces, where
past residents and former pre-presidents of the
general chicago community organize our school
like they learned at the school of the school of the
americas in the general chicago's dirty south side.
when the dirty south shows dirty wars with fresh
and absolute cleanliness, then we need to ask some
questions about our masks and weapons. not the
sweetness of this bitter crop, or that it kills us, but

how killing everything without killing all is ours, too,
so shit got to be sharper now. the general chicago's
general disbelief in anything and anybody got to get
sharper now, as that lil ol young thuggish murmur
turns to unfreaky executive action on al green, all
that handing grasped by bloody hands. see, it's the
cimarron condition of slabs and remnants, pepper

sauce on gristle, throb and grind, and all twisted
through the simple, necessary machine into some
doorways, a little moonlight, or some old and new

dreams about difference through surviving and living
on and on, and over, when somebody walks all up in
the image, 'cause why wouldn't some body take that
step, as if he's not your average huckleberry hound,
silver as how you look back at you from shining, big
pimping on, living that all over again, over and over
again? I mean, how can a subject not react like that
is how the union can't roll on like this, trying to be
some body killing all them trying not to kill nobody,
killing everybody, all but all mined in how he can't

kill us all, but all separate and enraged in this fucked up
western? the union are these stolen and essential services
when masters rape and eat servants all over the masterless
caribbean of tremor, desire and canal. it's not that we're
nonviolent, it's just that we love our flesh in danger and
revolt, and step back and kiss in heavy thump and gunfire,
since even the confusion we share is collectible, all taken
and gone and neither here nor there in the concept or the
thing or my old uncle henry down them dusty highways.
the new black art is this: find the self and make a killing.

I hope flesh and earth ain't the same as blood and soil
'cause I still can't stop. I'm gone with y'all even when
we separate and I'm in love with every little separate

gathering of our little all. I listen to that earthgang chili
sent me and I start crying. it sends me that he sent me
something to send me back to that earth, wind and fire
I be sending him all the time. it sends me back to lorna
goodison sending me back to nanny and I think about
emma amos and alma thomas and irma thomas and son
ford and kevin beasley'n'em and I can't stop flying home,

hoping that home and home ain't the same. we home
less, so I can hope, 'cause home, as you know, is where
the hatred is, all gathered in our little all as the various
things and selves we have to bring and sell. I'm all up
in that with y'all, even when I go off. it's just that we
got to talk about our masks and weapons. let's zoom
while we be dying, but not in the form of you and me,
'cause we can't protect our shit as if our running rules
the world. let's act a fool so dreamlike that the word
don't come. come on, now, let's hang out sometime.

let's tear up obligation in the way we pay attention. feel,
so we can talk about clyde taylor and amílcar cabral, the
mask of theory and the weapon of art, each one released
in the other's urgent holding as we renew the general
barbecue of the general chicago in the general tupelo,
honey, in the venereal swarm of our black funeral. who
can stop us on the road of this lovely dream beneath the
tree we hang from? who gon' stop us on this dust when
she's an angel of the last degree of freedom, eased on
down, through, gone, all foregiven in all that suasion?

it's all hers, as you know, though it could never all be hers
in tennessee. all she was was all betty and betty and bettye
and betty davis when she left his live, evil ass and moved to
louisville, up over the club, in a worn new bloom of return
to every night onstage in belo horizonte, um puoco sozinho,
'cause it ain't belong to her, 'cause she belonged to some
body. it ain't that she belonged to somebody, or that she
belong to us, or that what she gives can ever belong to us.
it's that share goes through her, and that we all broke that
way, and that we can't let that go, and that we got to hand

that on, that criticism is some company, a way of visiting,
a scary reminiscence on your porch or walking back 'cross
that field. this tendency to tend to nobody's business in
repose, which we steal from the work they steal, is always
on the edge. it has to love and it has to kill. it has to have
and be had and it has to tear away, and all that has to be
said over and over again as if it's never been said over and
over again in the gradually ragged incline of our sacrament.
we be climbing up the walls. what we share makes it hard
to talk about what we share. the physics can't be done by

number, and they be watching, and they give awards, and
one by one we got to live on that, and we all got to live
through all that, which is neither possible nor impossible
when your lover ain't around. it makes you want to figure
out the difference between you and me instead of letting
all that play out in the general chicago. what I want to say,
I and I, with love, in a way of letting all that oneness plea

and pli to numberless, is that this perversity is all outside
of all belonging, as all longing, in all need. y'all all I need
and I'm all gone in that, in that I gotta give y'all pleasure,

in that I'm so in love that all I do is disidentify, that all I
do is think about y'all all afternoon, and in the evening,
when the sun goes down, and in this slow taper toward
black night, rough outline, and common shawl. our fabric
is a ring of symbols; the sequins whirl like subterfuge on
black fire. criticism comps all this turbulence as we roll
the union on through massacre. I'm back in love and hate
again and I'm tired. can that we survive destroy what we
survive when we fall through equilibrium alive, across the
tracks, back 'cross that field, every time we turn around?

pando and medusa kinda feel like that, if the dirty south
were ancient greece in utah. can our blood corrode? can
the evening breeze tenderly abrade a settled metaphysics
to neither one nor many, like a trap set or an aspen grove,
cymbals fall and shimmer, cousin ethel and cousin mable
and val jeanty? sweet cotton is a bloody groove, a braid in
faulkner, mississippi, as the art of watching him watch us
watch his ass appraise. you think you alive when fighting
feels like fucking face-to-face? man, remember the drone
who works for the man who works for the drive is come

to steal your eye. he'll invade the place you make when
you get too old to be coming back every night to that
corner they run you off of every night. he'll say, "cool

breeze, common wind, have you seen jesse?" the treaty
of genocidal equilibrium often works all innocuous like
that. the pandemic keeps fucking with pandemonium
all ordinary and shit and in montana, where shit seem
obvious, the free individual's solitary confinement is
in stark opposition to that of the prisoner, as a coin
upside themselves: freedom and slavery, money and

winter in america. we celebrate that we survive so
we can kill what we survive, but black funereality
be mad sometimes at how it be surviving, which it
won't stop. frustrated by its own survival, which,
you know, it can't, it can't, it can't stop singing.
it breaks out (. . . .) in a cold sweat sometimes, and
then it just starts screaming, but then it says hold it
right there, and even there, right then, on the plot,
in the crypt, it wants some company, informal and
enforming spread and gather, sheaved to unobserve,

surreal, inside, upside, beyond, aboard, damn near
sometimes, as if bobby lee's little brother's boy and
erykah badu's baby daddy and I were the drells, one
on one in one with hourly sea nymphs, and the general
chicago just blur and burn all the way to oran, and we
call them back around from a scream to a whisper
and the whistle song's submarine dub in portmore
and houston and henderson and port henderson hill.
the general chicago is sky voile in lemon warehouse
and florida water is violet everglade. the dirty south

is a nigga cemetery. the dirty south is like decorations
in a nigga cemetery. since we got to be here, let's live,
dying of how we live better than them all open, close,
come by and lose in tone, keen, unquantized, j dilla'd
as a valvedrum, screw'd, dj'd, trade blue mud in whorl
gone bluiett and subnaval in this infinite consanguinity
passing through. mystique, motherfucker? déséquilibre!
meanwhile, blackness—apparently none as the air we
surface, urge, and till; all out from under the war of
understanding—is some hand held out, approaching.

asé

achieving
the fullness
of my sub
jectivity
was hard;
maintaining
it is harder.
whole lotta
motherfuckers
been killed.

let me be
fully myself
and say I've killed
a whole lotta
motherfuckers.

the shit is
beautiful.
feel the
private feel
of all this
brutal privacy.

in spite of
everything,
a little of
which now
I can call
my own,
is how I
got here.

cowreckd and led to trespass

retroit locticians are logicians
proving autocorrect incorrect
with every twist and turn and
village ghetto land and chapel
plane and little offline slant, a
verb! your tress be practicing!

finger printing

this is transcendental bruise
research, and shade research
recess, caresscavation, and a
kind of lining, but I sent to say,
but I meant to say meant to
say mining, made of giving,
but I meant to say all these
things, being all thumbs,
which is to ask, after the
brushwork of your thumbs,
after the sense of shade by
hand, mbir, and sacrament
of open-handed application.

these notes on finger painting
note how the refusal to separate
finger and painting is over
rubbed into finger printing,
dancing in emma's "high water
mark" everywhere, which keeps
noticing nothing so nearly, so
nere, son de early morning
sun, annotating neither here
nor there in general smudge
and march and lineated dinge,

and a depression of children's
lakes full of wildly divergent
arches and little pegs of ribbon,
rhythm, strand, and water
music, that I thought, ashon's
thoughts on nothing music!

so, here's some being sent
by way of introduction.

taj subduction

the way we live now is a map of living won't approach

but today, with my friend, in artery,
     we meet who've grown from bodies, we surface scientists of sound, we pray seawall window, we feel we feel together,

we got so much work to do, we need to go outside and play.

     as witness, we can't be the opposite.
locks touch the ground like tentacles in spray.
     now, we see the sylphs have come to light.
     what if we talk with us of what we see, with how we see this move through ordered air in tore-up song.

that's breathturn, right, pierre? irregular salon come incorrect. we talk with what we see, right, jean-pierre?

existence is arboreal, then menus emerge.

lopez lopes. cleaver cleaves.

without corinna, sho' don't mean, sho' don't mean a nachel thang.

subductive lauren

think for fight for
here ain't here yet. fly
for there, think of that,
what if beautiful horizon.
if obscure contour ask
me now, aside in velvet
lounge, is surface séance?
sound like that's our
next strange chance.

with the band$_2$

'cause ain't no wall for
ground and atmosphere
if the instrument is soft
shoe or conceptual sax
in perpetual drumstick
or hard little paintbrush.
black + blue or blur or
blood or bruise + brath
waite on a glenn black
beach arrange intimate
nonlocalities of pigment,
medium, material, and
surfacing, anawaiting
unarrive as singing kicks
up dust and muck on fire.
singe extends the shit
in acutely obtuse angels
of the undegreed, burns
laid out, inlaid outpour
and aspirant powder to
new, incandent soothe.
chant or tjant for tjosh
regardless, recumbent
in recombinant horizon.
start some raspy, nasty,

meschant tanzen on duet's
eventually january bloom
and clouj. ozdjhe, obese,
unshorn & reforgotten clef,
step off, unlock, then fry.

why you leave 'em with me?

pas de dull,
shade-prefaced letter begging and little bump accusations,
post-facial portraitures and black citational businesses, and
no actual doing of the bump despite the continual posting
of pictures of musicians drugged in the drake-like not quite
making of the music, selfies documenting the pas de duck
like liteness of this dual not taking care, this dull, careless,
half-duetish talking 'bout care all the goddamn time in all
this selfish disavowal of selflessness you be doing together
all by yourselves when you take the measure of the world.
whatever. it's better ones at it anyway, doin' two to death
with museum quality, hung in the remodeled mid-century
modern house party. how many blocks away you say you
live? can I come get some frozen shrimp? oh, ok. no more
letters. I'm gone, but you better stop fucking with fumi.

                                    not applicable,
here s'more + less than additive rescriptions of down
laid, motile incompletenessing, muscularity of ba-lues
are brewin's bent madrigal. come get some but neither
watch nor witness ensemble's dissembling renewal and
review. preformative presentuosity's radical compliqué
lets all the deviance of all the word have it all its own
way. the aromatic unfolding of the book we're writing
is gregarious—neremitic but floral in shared seclusion
and long look and a green feather and some blue tape
on a little head fresh cut by miss irene. this ornament
of open secret easter is paraprofessional; and payback
is impossible, as you say. we owe each other all that,
too. but each and other, y'all say that shit y'all say
all by y'allself, so long, it's sunday, that's the day.

got 'im!

other little
man white
is a gator
got trapped
in a garbage
can, roll
down to
the pond
and release.
know what?
call a realtor,
get up out
from there.
your house is
in the damn
pond. really,
it ain't even
your house
so fuck a
realtor, just
get your shit
and go. or
just go, shit.

merda nostra

our shit?
—delays
choice in
definitely
in double
  silt in
finitude

knotting

the knot
obliterates
inside out,
literalizing
inside out
so that
beautiful
questions
appear to
reappear.
we speak
of knot
or knots
instead of
speaking in
knotting.
to speak of
knotting,
say while
knitting,
induces calm.
aw, but the
heavy roil
of speaking
in knotting!
beautiful
questions
disappear
in hand.

epistrophe and epistrophy

some ekphrastic evening, this'll be both criticism and poetry and
failing that fall somewhere that seems like in between. this both/
and and/or neither/nor machine comes in having been touched
by what's seen and wanting to touch what's seen through some
extraordinary realities. it has to do with what's heard in what's
shown: the rolling air of nevermade nonet's everyday recording,

unraveled scrolls, hung from rather than placed on their support,
are partially let go and let touch the ground and, more loosely
and informally than the brokenplace book usually allows, touch
one another. this semi-floored unfurl of volume is imprevisionary
light. the epistrophic is a scene it seems like we can't help but want
to touch. it turns out and back on itself into the end of the book's
endless history. moreover, we're foregiven what it is to see with
and through to what it represents, since mimesis just can't let go
transparent dreams. the gliss on this is like organza, clarity fatal as
reflection to seeing with and seeing through, which are felt oblique
and pressed against, unpointed, hand-painted, the very palpable
touch preservation wants to guard against. guardedness in blue
museology is what epistrophe all but guardedly defies. so, shahzia
says, nothing's hidden by these draperies; what's hidden by them
hides and then something happens when hiding is seen and seen
through, and veiling as revealing is embraced and refused. scrolls
of shifting border off familiarities in phases of successive phrases,

epistrophe, aka epiphora, anaphora's counterpart or counterpoint,
indicating turning about, twisting things or affairs, but also moving

up and down, is engineered from *epi*, or upon, and *strophe*, turning,
whose proto-indo-european rootlessness is "to wind" in rhetoric
and figure, which successive phrases follow with that same word,

to affirm. it's also used in music, though affirmation, as when a band
turns out from and back onto and through and with itself to abolish
jubilee, a common wind of tone kept coming back to itself as other
than itself, as other than beginning or end in epistrophy, says epistrophe,
as if again and again we show how falling is rising turned and turning
about turning in fair play and coming out right in consensual simplicity,
in reversal of upon unto draping what hangs about us like a garment,
marking flesh's closeness to clothing and the whole textilic field of
textual welcome, where skin falls into skein's release of parchment,
resonant with this relaxation of curling rosamond brings on tilled,
preleased, deciduous, and aviarily undecidable reliefs of leaf and wing.
in wind and leave, epistrophe is seen and heard as sheet music, as a music

of tresses, of dressage in undress, or unrest in and under the duress of
brutal, incompetent determination—a transcript of wind all unwound
before and after. epiphora means carry on, or bear, or persist, or suffer,
or endure, and it's not surprising that it can't quite do what it means
as it also stands, on the cusp of matter and emotion, for the presence
of a watering eye, tearing inseparable from tearing, a little overflow
of tears whose tracks tear up the portrait of composure with more
and less than normal crying. epistrophe, by way of what repeats it
differently, flowers into overflowing, flown and overflown in pianistic
lágrima, orchid, moth. is eyewatering, like mouthwatering, a function
of appetite? is it like when a particular sensual experience makes another
sense go off? if so, it's not the experience but its denial that prompts
and urges. in this anasynaesthetic mood, I'm crying for what I shouldn't

touch. I'm touched, in this regard. in this regard, I am impassioned.
I'm with y'all dragging witness's sad spectatorial drag of all involved.
involvement in pansensual ravishing and unraveling of regard is epistrophe
accompanied by anaphora, which epiphora carries at its root, even when

anaphora's not there, even when epistrophe and epiphora are displaced.
repetition is dis place/meant, too, and sometimes almost means avoid,
as in the case of fold tending not to turn toward self-enveloping. it's like
a repeated end making up so insistently for the absence of its repeated
beginning that beginning come out to show them in the end. anaphora,
the repetition of a word or phrase in the beginning of successive clauses,
is derived from *anapherein*, carrying back, or bringing up, from *ana*, back,
+ *pherein*, all to bear. this cutback cuts against the wave it rides, cutting
together-apart in tuned negation, till it seems like anaphora is present in
epistrophe, jut like wounding, turning, falling, and bearing are all up in
epistrophy. and all we want is nothing come first and nothing come before
we just want to be none in being-involved and therefore ample, unalone,
and nonaligned in movement, fumi bending birdy-like precision in band
or bandung, not in search but in coral refusal of the one as karen carols
all this anaphoric, epistrophic play of carry in soft, urgent conferencing
and carting, and roopnaraine cartering, and alissa andaiyeing, ah ndiya
ah demiurge, breathe simurgh with catastrophic joy, and turn and turn

the falling page. all involved's symphatic chorograph, as epistrophe and
epistrophy repeat their saturation of repletion, as issey rehearsing isaïe
singing holland's tilted river, as shahzia's revenant breeze reciting monk
reversing drawn out tuck and tranche, as the union rolls on and on and
incomplete in unending counteropenings of seem and seam and seme,
our plea folds like a dream of the guianas, where the real is for the people.

or discovering

this clean, perdurant sheet is our music.
the billowing square deforms and then it falls
close to square, something like diminished
being something like enlarged, and this enfolding,
not unfolding like a story but riding in
this general involvement in the story,
where aunt kine be hollering at lisa every day,
a roll of common roil or sail or shook
toil, a scroll of paint on paint in paint,
all carefully installed in the keno house
of her kino-eye. aunt kine and edward kienholz,
and bond, who is discovered in being covered, and
vertov furl and toss and stirreth like a nest

or something cooked down low in birdsong
when the plot thickens and bottom buckles
air with clotted alouette. all that grumbling
in the arrant nave; all rough into existence
as we make an edge and discompose
whatever will have posed in fictive standing.
in this regardless turning on regard,

the homotopic says I'm not the one,
　　but it couldn't relate, it couldn't relate,
it couldn't relate. the physics of it shuns
　　the metaphysics, which is given in the figure
　　　of the one, which the no-count turn upon
　　　　　themself in stolen moments of conception.
　　our koan is a gesture of commencement
　　and wave overtakes the elevated hand.
　　aware in pouring, unaware of selves,
　　　the homotopic gathers in dispersion,

whose measurement is always more and less
in measure. just like memory in club
　　rouge, or in the worn, undamaged river,
let's stay preliminary in our practice.

graves say, grave says

1.

drumming is martial art,
trap set to touch, is soca
in your waist, you got a
gun up in your waist. in
the four brush chambers
of shaolin and blackwell
heart, in l'rosen avenue,
in explode in lil dis & lil
dat all goddamn day —

at the end of the word at the end of the world,
a mermaid in a boxcar lay some track on some
long, unlonesome seed, driving trap thorough
milespace, at milespace, little buzzard undone

insideout, and we are young again, contraption, in a ship and shimmering ride of charles gaines trees.

that point-to-point
navigation all dead
subjects have to want

and want to want be
cause you can't
be somebody if

you can't be someplace, which is the corner of dead and
new, just got tore up by some non-local transintensities.

braid this concern for the music —
which is braided with an ability
not to read the music, which is
a way to braid away pure sound —

with how we breathe and ground not in between the music and our rhetoric,
when the music is our rhetoric's surround, asway, in reprecision bitter suite.

one track don't make no sense.

many don't make none neither.

you hear the solo solo as
solo, deictic wish + one.

to defend the trappist right to be oneself is some deep hate, sista fool yourself, so you can have one.

come on, let's let that go in new mass eccentricity.

where it's at ain't nowhere, in some of neverywhere, nevada of the fabricant dust, where fabric is the gathered dust of tearing, of involvement with shearing, of concern with dis emplot/meant's misconception, of apposition in apportion.

repercussion is terrible, beautiful, yes, yes, I know

2.

seem like here and there,
bebe's finale or b's other
hand, always be under re
view. but b, what I want

to say — you know — you
know — is that it can't be
about some bullshit shift
from bop policing to de
stituent freedom. o, the
merylic tic! mad at ain't
mad enough, all sad and
timid, lil yts sad groove,

a such a thing so lacks the chance to feed
to show that history needs supple meant

and we want to hear how drummers keep not giving sum. in theft of turn and come,

of let and go when ain't no going back, when ain't no let off, no getting here or there, no getting out of it, no getting
    anything out of all our little all
been stolen, all and all brutally gotten out of, out of us all thrown away, arreal up under all the air of all that memory
    in the air of our garage on fire.

insofar as we're in so far,
to refuse the murderous
derivative is nothing but
driven rhythm in design.

"computer" is none ÷ one who cipher,
insuring the shipped ain't no accident.
that's that common sheer we shipped
all see through — so we say, we're the
matter, boss: we shipped. *we* shipped.
max, we the matrix at the heart of matter.

to your batterie, we blow! shit sound like song got thrown in drowned thriving.

3.

on a rift, off track, intraaction. our sophonic
réel-to-réel's palimpseste fantastique's drowned software,
canehol'd data, and computative cotton is that goodlooking sound.

financial instrument, the zero degree of 808 is furrowed arbitrage
and mountainous, comps various air, breaks relation and abandon,
absorbing life and code and frustrate touch where hand or stick on
skin, in recoil and again and difference engineered, remind us that

the heartbeat of the beaten to death can't be unheard in the music.
burning flesh in the music. prepared table get turned in the music.
actuarial flow in the music whether you don't like the music or do
I do. what you do. oh when I do. my love to you, lil dream lil dog.

it's middle bypass, and cpr in cpt, insovereign hanksync's soft machine caress. thrown hands give breath to pulse
in plain seed, in botany and architecture, in epicurean landscape, in anatomism's black rock book, motherfucker,

for you have but mistook us all this while.
scholarly clerk, ain't nothing in your way.

perennial fashion
is fly
in the open diary

tentacular message, comprise flavored listening, release phantom weight, extract the labor of extracting shift or
    caramel from endless rows of stalks
or vines or tones of moves or static lines of jailed assemblies, tell time and space, purr imaginary numbers, give
    us goosebumps, tentacular massage,

hear?   not here.   grave says.

        no there,   graves say,   offline and asymptotic and simple

in our inbalance
is fly
presence falling

acknowledgments

Versions of some of these poems have appeared in the exhibition catalogs *Carrie Mae Weems: A Great Turn in the Possible*, *The Dirty South: Contemporary Art, Material Culture, and the Sonic Impulse*, *Foundation for Contemporary Arts 2021*, *Heard Immunity: Poems and Pictures Now*, *Imagine Freedom: Art Works for Abolition*, *Kevin Beasley: A view of a landscape*, and *Milford Graves: A Mind-Body Deal*; in the journals *Conjunctions*, *Jazz and Culture*, *Magma*, and *The Volta*; as liner notes for the sound recording *Braids* by Sam Rivers; and as sound recordings on the album *Moten/López/Cleaver*. Many thanks to the artists, curators, and editors involved.